JOINT VENTURES IN MEXICO

Robert J. Radway

[AMA Management Briefing]

AMA MEMBERSHIP PUBLICATIONS DIVISION   1985
AMERICAN MANAGEMENT ASSOCIATIONS

Library of Congress Cataloging in Publication Data

Radway, Robert J., 1940-
  Joint ventures in Mexico.

  (AMA management briefing)
  1. Joint ventures—Mexico.   I. Title.   II. Series.
  Law   346.72'068   82-13773
  ISBN 0-8144-2273-X   347.20668

© 1984 AMA Membership Publications Division

American Management Associations, New York.

This Management Briefing has been distributed to all members enrolled in the International Division of the American Management Associations. Copies may be purchased at the following single-copy rates: AMA members, $7.50. Non-members, $10.00. Students, $3.75 (upon presentation of a college/university identification card at an AMA bookstore). Faculty members may purchase 25 or more copies for classroom use at the student discount rate (order on college letterhead).

First Printing

About the Author

Robert J. Radway is a founding partner of Radway & Dalto, a New York law firm specializing in international business transactions, primarily those relating to the market penetration strategies of U.S. companies abroad but also including representation of foreign companies in a similar manner in the U.S.

Before establishing his own practice in 1978, Mr. Radway spent several years as inside counsel with high technology companies. He later served as legal adviser of the Council of the Americas, monitoring all changes in laws and regulations affecting U.S. companies doing business in Latin America.

Spanning a period of over 20 years, Mr. Radway's legal and business experience has involved the establishment of agent/distributor relationships, licenses, branches, subsidiaries, and joint ventures abroad, and the preparation of proposals/contracts from feasibility through project completion for large turnkey plant construction. His work involves direct negotiations with high- and middle-level government officials in Mexico, Brazil, Venezuela, and other Latin American countries, as well as in Europe and the Far East, bringing him into close contact with the business and economic life of these countries. Increasingly, he has been called upon to assist in locating qualified partners for joint venture investments in Latin American countries, particularly Mexico, and to offer general business and legal advice on joint ventures abroad.

Mr. Radway received his BBA and MBA from the University of Michigan and his JD from the University of California, Hastings College of the Law. He is active in bar associations and the Licensing Executives Society and has lectured on joint ventures, transfer of technology, foreign investments, and related subjects in Europe and throughout the Western Hemisphere. In addition, he is the author of numerous law and business journal articles analyzing laws and practices of the Latin American countries. He is coauthor/editor of the *Reference Manual on Doing Business in Latin America* and has served as an adviser to major publications of Oceana and Clark Boardman in these fields and serves as a consultant to specialized agencies of the United Nations in matters regarding multinational corporations in developing countries. In February, 1984, he was elected to the Council of the Inter-American Bar Association.

Contents

Introduction

Mexico has again become one of the most attractive countries in the world for U.S. companies to do business with—or in. Such factors as its 3,000 kilometer border with the U.S., its proximity to U.S. transportation, its increasingly higher skilled (and currently low-wage) labor force, and taxes that apply only to the value added in Mexico have led to the creation of a highly successful in-bond assembly and manufacturing industry to produce goods for the U.S. market. Indeed, Canadian, European, and Japanese companies are now deriving economic benefits from this *maquiladora* industry. The spillover effect from the high-technology companies established in that program is just beginning to impact on the local markets in Mexico, but the possibilities are intriguing. Whatever the business (licensing, the provision of technical, financial, or consulting services, or involvement in assembly or manufacture through direct investment), North American companies of virtually all sizes and from all industries are "rediscovering Mexico," and an increasing number are in a position to reap benefits from the joint venture challenge.

Mexico is in a transition period. In 1982, three devaluations, the imposition of unfamiliar exchange controls, and the nationalization of private Mexican banks rocked Mexican and foreign investors alike. The first year of the six-year *(sexennio)* term of

President Miguel de la Madrid Hurtado was relatively successful in taking the first few steps (in a journey of 1,000 miles) toward restoring confidence and recovering the impressive growth rates Mexico had realized from 1946 until 1981. That first year (1983) ended with Mexico realizing a significant trade surplus, primarily through sharp cutbacks in imports. Negative growth was registered in 1982 and 1983, but projections for 1984, 1985, and beyond begin to look more healthy.

Many are asking whether the recession and financial (debt) crisis has resulted in any structural changes in the economy. It became clear that serious efforts were under way to substitute locally produced raw materials and parts for imports, and the beginning of a real awareness of the necessity to be export competitive emerged. Many companies took the opportunity to trim excess fat and improve efficiency. Others went bankrupt. The Mexican State (through the bank "nationalization") swelled to nearly three-fourths of the productive sector of the economy, then began to face the need to reprivatize. This also meant that many foreign companies now had the Mexican government as their joint venture partner, a relationship that often required changes in strategy.

Once again, North American, European, and Japanese investors began to clarify their vision of Mexico as one of the richest countries in the world in metallic and nonmetallic minerals and hydrocarbons, with a population of about 75 million inhabitants that is continuing to grow.

In late 1984, realizing that at least one to two years is required to lay the foundation for a successful joint venture, foreign investors began to reassess their strategic assumptions in Mexico and move forward into the next growth period.

OFFENSIVE VS. DEFENSIVE

As every executive knows, there are offensive and defensive marketing strategies. Because Mexican law places all foreign investors in the position of minority partners within joint ventures, many U.S. firms have adopted a defensive strategy—and a defensive mentality. Moreover, the Mexican market, lucrative as it may be, presents an extremely complex and difficult environment in which to operate. This frequently leads to an inadequate allocation of managerial time and other resources. Coupled with an equally inadequate understanding of the problems at hand, this weakness interferes with the attainment of greater profits, higher productivity, and better continuity in operations.

U.S. executives must overcome their reluctance to recruit, train, and indoctrinate bright, talented younger Mexicans to assume greater control and management responsibility. In the past, the basic character of Mexican corporate strategy, and the foreigner's inclination to bring in expatriate managers rather than develop Mexican management, added to a profile that eventually hampered operations. Rather, U.S. executives must make every effort to see Mexican business through Mexican eyes—an essential part of their commitment to the profitable operation of the joint venture. Only through an adequate and ongoing commitment can this most complex form of business entity be successfully adapted to a most complex business culture.

A LOOK AHEAD

This monograph will be directed first at the problems foreign companies already established in Mexico face in transforming into a joint venture, then at the issues involved in establishing new companies in the joint venture form. Manufacturing companies will be treated first, and then companies providing services, particularly architecture, design, engineering, construction, and construction management or related types of "contractual services."

Readers are advised, however, to read the entire monograph, not just those chapters pertaining to areas of individual interest. The opening chapter, for example, discusses the chain of events leading up to the implementation of the Foreign Investment Law and the impact this law and related policy has had on foreign investment. The second chapter, dealing with joint ventures in manufacturing, offers seasoned advice on finding the right partner. One of several critical success factors discussed in the monograph, the partnership issue has implications for other forms of investment as well. The third chapter includes discussion of some of the tax implications associated with providing certain services. These tax consequences frequently attach to manufacturing ventures as well, and are issues faced equally by pre-existing companies or new entrants.

1

Companies Previously Established in Mexico

THE FOREIGN INVESTMENT LAW AND ITS OBJECTIVES

On March 9, 1973, the Law to Promote Mexican Investment and to Regulate Foreign Investment (hereafter the Foreign Investment Law or FIL) was published in the official *Gazette* and became effective on May 8 of that year. The culmination of over five decades in the evolution of Mexican policy, the FIL was intended to consolidate Mexico's economic independence by promoting national investment, stimulating a fair and balanced development, and controlling foreign investment. Indeed, it is impossible to talk about any form of foreign investment without knowledge of the major elements of this legislation.

To appreciate the background, one should understand something of the historic role of foreign investment in Mexico. Suffice it to mention that foreign capital in Mexico, as in many other developing countries, had frequently entered through highly visible industries, which became the targets of criticism during periods of national crisis. Foreign capital played an especially important role in mining and infrastructure during the dictatorship of Porfirio Diaz until 1910 and the outbreak of the Mexican Revolution.

In 1917, a new Constitution was prepared and accepted, containing the blueprint to increase the control held by Mexicans over the industrialization process of their nation. In the early years after the revolution, Mexico ranked second in oil production among world nations. Tension between the foreign companies controlling production and the Petroleum Workers' Union, strengthened by the revolution and subsequent events, led to the nationalization of the oil properties on March 18, 1938, and the establishment of *Petroleos Mexicanos* (PEMEX) as a state-owned oil company. The previous year had witnessed the final nationalization of the railroads, exactly 100 years after Emperor Maximilian had initiated the first railroad from Mexico City to Veracruz.

During the early 1940s, a different emphasis emerged. Spurred by the effects of World War II and a consequent reduction in imports, government leaders attempted to direct foreign capital into production for domestic consumption. After the war and through the 1950s, a policy began to evolve of attracting foreign capital and technology to supplement Mexican capital. In 1960, the electric power companies were nationalized into the state-owned *Corporacion Federal de Electricidad* (CFE) with no significant disruption to foreign investment, and the now well-known import substitution policies engulfed Mexico and all of Latin America throughout the 1960s. Several important decrees, passed in 1970, 1971, and 1972, continued the trend toward reserving certain industries to the state and to Mexican investors, thus laying the foundation for the Foreign Investment Law.

The first article of the FIL states that its purpose is to "promote Mexican investment and regulate foreign investment in order to stimulate a just and balanced development and consolidate the country's economic independence." Foreign investment, therefore, was declared to be welcome as long as it helped to achieve the country's objectives—that is, as long as it served to complement national investment but not to displace existing business enterprises operating satisfactorily.

Mexico's national development goals, formulated in the wake of a population growth rate of 3.5 percent at the outset of the 1970s, anticipated the need for a rate of capital formation that would keep the gross domestic product (GDP) growing faster than the population. Only through such growth could industry absorb the expanding workforce and keep a lid on Mexico's potentially serious social problems. Foreign capital and technology were given an important role in fueling these great engines.

In order to develop the infrastructure to accommodate this industrial expansion, energy (hydrocarbons in particular) was identified as the most critical element. Advances in oil extraction technology and a modification and acceleration of exploration activity coincided with the sharp increase in international oil prices in 1973-74 to support the conclusion that oil would be the key to Mexico's economic growth.

But the condition of Mexico's infrastructure, as then assessed by Mexican planners, left much to be improved. The transportation system had been in place essentially unmodified since the end of the last century, including a single-track railroad geared strictly to shipping basic agricultural and mining commodities to port for export. The ports themselves were totally inadequate. These facilities simply could not handle the imports needed to fuel the industrial expansion or the exports of oil and nontraditional manufactured and agricultural items that would pay for the increased import of machinery and equipment. Moreover, the electric power requirements needed by the year 2000 were enormous, calling for huge increases in conventional and nuclear power generation capacity as well as transmission and distribution lines to feed the country. Corresponding internal transportation and communication networks did not exist in much of the country.

Finally, years of spiraling population growth rates and inadequate income in rural areas had contributed to the familiar urban migration problem suffered by industrialized and developing countries alike. Mexico's population has been increasingly concentrated in its three major urban and industrial areas: Mexico City (including the Federal District), Guadalajara, and Monterrey—the industrial Pittsburgh of the north. The planners were determined to find ways of deconcentrating the population into agricultural, coastal, and other soon-to-be-growing industrial areas (especially those with proximity to natural resources that could be developed and processed). The plans that were formulated attempted to ease the heavy burden resting on the urban centers and redistribute income in a country with vivid distinctions between rich and poor, and only recent beginnings of a middle class.

Capital goods were identified early as a high-priority industry to be developed to fuel the industrial expansion. This determination evolved through the 1970s, since the oil revenues had to be spread around to meet social and economic objectives. President Lopez Portillo referred to this process as "planting the oil," a conversion of a nonrenewable resource into a more coordinated basis for the country's development. Agriculture was also identified as a high-priority sector, although the limited percentage of tillable land in Mexico, coupled with a natural water problem and an impractical and unproductive agrarian reform program (the *ejido* system which was incorporated into their 1917 Constitution), posed a formidable constraint to accomplishing the objective of agricultural self-sufficiency.

Throughout all this was an underlying concern for avoiding foreign dominance or control of the national industrial apparatus, through either equity participation or actual management or control of Mexican business operations.

IMPLEMENTATION OF FIL OBJECTIVES: MEXICANIZATION

There were, therefore, two major objectives to be implemented with the FIL and its policy: (1) channeling of new investment into those sectors that the law identified as open to foreign participation and (2) gradually transferring a considerable amount of pre-FIL investment into the hands of Mexicans (known as Mexicanization) to accomplish the stated objectives. Article Twelve of the FIL provided the National Foreign Investment Commission (NFIC) with the authority to determine the percentages of foreign investment's participation in the country's different geographical areas and in those economic activities that were not otherwise regulated by other specific statutes. Article Thirteen provided a criteria for the NFIC to consider in making such determinations with respect to new investment and the expansion of existing investment.

It was well known that over 2,500 companies existed that were essentially 100 percent foreign owned. Because Mexico has a strong tradition against retroactive application of its laws, these companies were not immediately obliged to transform (or divest) to equity levels below 50 percent. The right to remain wholly foreign owned after the passage of the FIL is commonly termed a "grandfather" right. The presence of these companies, however, pervaded virtually every sector of economic activity in the country, with the exception of those reserved to the state or to purely Mexican capital.

The expressed purpose of Mexicanization is to transfer control of Mexico's industrial establishment to the hands of Mexican equity investors. In this regard, the stated desire was that decisions at ownership and operating levels were to be made as much as possible by Mexican nationals with Mexican national interests in mind. It was believed that Mexican nationals would identify more closely with social and economic constraints of the republic than would foreign nationals.

The policymakers determined that Mexicanization would be implemented most effectively through transformation of three major components: equity capital, management, and control. Articles Four and Five of the FIL set forth limitations on foreign equity capital to a maximum of 49 percent as a general matter, and lower in specified areas (secondary petrochemicals, for example, automotive parts, and certain strategic mining properties). Article Five contained corresponding provisions that such percentage of foreign capital should not be empowered by any means to determine the management of the business. It also provided that the participation of foreigners in the management of the business could not exceed its equity participation.

Enforcing the objectives with respect to control would prove to be more complicated. This would be undertaken through the administrative mechanisms of the bureau in the designated ministry (Secretariat of Commerce and Industrial Development), which was empowered to issue the permits required for an increasing number of industrial activities in Mexico.

APPROACH TO MEXICANIZATION OF PRE-EXISTING FOREIGN COMPANIES

The Mexicanization policy of the NFIC, implemented through the bureau and other departments of commerce and other ministries, can be seen in three distinct periods: (1) from mid-1973 through the end of 1978, (2) from the publication in 1979 of the National Industrial Development Plan (NIDP) to the end of November, 1982, and (3) from December 1, 1982, to the present.

Senior government officials anticipated that foreign businesses would grow through either expansion, relocation, or acquisition; specific provisions of the law were drafted with this in mind. Articles Eight and Twelve of the FIL addressed expansion through both the acquisition of an increasing percentage of an existing Mexican enterprise (discussed below), or through intrinsic growth through one of four means: extending existing operations to the same customers (new establishments), developing new lines of products, initiating new lines of business (economic activities), and serving new markets or new customers.

Expansion

Resolution 8, issued in 1975, further regulated foreign investment in new establishments, in particular, those establishments designed to expand existing operations to serve growth needs of existing customers. The resolution adopted a "physically independent and distinct" test to determine what constituted a new establishment. Thus, a relocation would satisfy the test, as would a new physical undertaking without regard to the legal or financial structuring of the transaction and designation of the new physical unit. Exceptions were made for purely administrative and warehousing activities that were more mechanical in nature than profit centers.

New lines of products and new economic activities were further regulated by Resolution 16, enacted in 1977. With that pronouncement, the NFIC established an itemized summary of economic activities of product lines (including services) divided into groups, subgroups, and classes. If the new activity, product, or service fell within a classification different from the activities previously carried out on a commercial scale on an ongoing daily basis, the test was met.

Resolution 16 also addressed expansion through serving new markets or customers. Among other factors, this resolution considered the identity of the consumers to be served, the price of the new product or service, and the relevant market or customer group and characteristics that would differentiate it from the specific market previously serviced. Meeting any of the tests defined above would, therefore, require specific approval in the form of a permit from the NFIC.

In addressing expansion through relocations, Resolutions 8 and 15 applied some of the criteria from Article Thirteen of the law itself, such as the contribution that the relocation would make to industrial decentralization and employment opportunities in less-developed zones of the country. These criteria presaged the strong emphasis on decentralization later to be defined in the 1979 NIDP. According to Resolution 15, relocation of commercial, administrative, or service establishments could be approved by the executive secretary of the NFIC in two principal cases: first, if the relocation was within the same state and did not involve an expansion of greater than 20 percent of the establishment being relocated, and second, a relocation could be made to a different state in the republic if the expansion did not exceed 40 percent and the relocation was carried out to a zone of relatively lower stage of economic development. Otherwise NFIC approval would be required.

Acquisitions

Resolution 11, issued in 1976, attempted to clarify the authorization requirements for acquisitions of more than 25 percent of the capital or 49 percent of the fixed assets of an existing Mexican enterprise by foreign investors. Leasing of the enterprise or the essential assets was considered equivalent to outright acquisition. Also requiring authorizations under the law were transactions by which foreign investors acquired the rights to manage the enterprise. Conceivably, this would encompass a management contract, which is also subject to approval under the companion Transfer of Technology Law, effective in early 1973 and revised in 1982.

Since Mexico has a strong tradition against *ex-post facto* legislation, suggestions were made that an acquisition of a small percentage of equity or assets, when added to previous holdings, would exceed the levels set forth in the law. Mexican lawyers took the position that this was an unconstitutional attempt to apply this law retroactively. The NFIC responded through Resolution 11, clarifying that the law, as regulated, applied to the effects of the current transaction when meeting the defined test, thereby safely passing the legal challenge.

A new wrinkle was introduced in late 1981, however, through the publication of an amended Resolution 11 aimed at curtailing that process commonly known as "pyramiding of enterprises"— a tactic in which foreign investors, acting through their 49 percent interest in a Mexican company, acquire a 51 percent interest in a new joint venture. More on this later.

Second Stage

With the publication in 1979 of the NIDP, the Mexicanization policy evolved in a new direction. The coordination with the industrial plan (and the various incentive decrees issued thereafter) became apparent almost immediately. The NIDP redefined and clarified the country's earlier development objectives. Although the government's National Energy Program was not issued until late 1980, the essential elements were known to the planners when the NIDP was issued. In fact, early in 1980 a Global Development Plan was presented to the executive, legislative, and judicial branches of the Mexican government by the then minister of programming and budgeting, Lic. Miguel de la Madrid Hurtado, later to become the next president of the republic. The Global Plan contains some ambitious economic objectives, built around the NIDP and a series of specific plans for food (agriculture), housing, urban development, transportation, energy, and other significant elements of the country's ambitious program.

Once again, energy (both oil and electric power generation) became the centerpiece. Other strategic industries were those judged to be most important in the accomplishment of social and economic development goals: agriculture/food processing and capital goods, for example. From that point forward, Mexicanization policy was aimed at supporting those foreign companies that complied with NIDP goals.

Third Stage

The financial (debt) crisis emerged in 1981-82 amidst local claps of thunder, followed by lightning that struck four times during 1982—the three devaluations of the Mexican peso (February, August, and December) and the September 1, 1982, back-to-back decrees establishing exchange controls and nationalizing the private Mexican banks. Because of the crisis and the accompanying shortage of liquidity (aggravated by an extensive pattern of capital flight due to the erosion of confidence), Mexican government planners were forced to reassess the Mexicanization policy. Officials determined that there was a critical need to increase the inflow of capital—shoring up the current account to meet newly restructured debt service obligations and helping to restore confidence.

Attracting foreign capital thus became a higher economic priority, despite its attendant political difficulties. Along with this challenge (which generally requires some assurances of stability and growth potential) emerged a realization that the liquidity shortage would mean fewer Mexican investors available to acquire shares of foreign-owned companies. In addition, and of no small consequence, was the government's major effort to reprivatize the nonbanking operations of the now state-owned banks. The capital market was too thin, and something had to give.

Not only did the Mexicanization policy yield to these pressures (at least for the time being), but a few U.S. companies were given express permission to repurchase shares in their local affiliates that had been Mexicanized during the 10 years since the FIL had become effective.

Finally, on February 17, 1984, after much discussion, the Secretary of Commerce and Industrial Development announced a new set of guidelines ("Guidelines on Foreign Investment and Reasons Behind Promotion of Same"), which contained some important policy pronouncements. In summary, the NFIC would consider approval of up to 100 percent foreign ownership in the 34 categories designated as priorities in the guidelines, in return for satisfaction of criteria to be determined in each case. Although the criteria would vary and be tailored to industry, technology, local demand, and competitive factors, it generally included higher local content (that is, import substitution), exports at least to compensate for imports (offset plus), attraction of key technology designed to strengthen the Mexican economy in the weaker priority areas, and, of course, decentralization and job creation as previously stressed. Indeed, it was anticipated that in all of these cases a vague future commitment to Mexicanize would also be required.

Other administrative changes were announced that had not yet been implemented six months later, and early results were (except for very high technology situations) indicative that, despite an apparently major policy shift from the cabinet level, the middle-level technocrats had dug in and were not about to give away what had been jealously constructed for the previous 10 years. Key personnel changes also suggested that the ever-present internal policy struggle was not yet won by those favoring fewer restrictions on foreign investment—not by a long shot!

MECHANICS OF MEXICANIZATION

The 1979 NIDP contained a shopping list of incentives, referred to as tools for accomplishing the plan, and made these incentives available to companies that contributed to the plan's execution. For companies seeking to establish themselves in the newly defined zones of economic priorities, the plan offered discounts of up to 30 percent in energy supplies (gas, oil, electric power, and the like) and petrochemical products.

Also offered were tax credits, investment credits, job creation credits, financial preferences, and favorable accounting treatment for those companies complying. At the same time, the NIDP imposed some export requirements (commitment on the part of the new enterprise to export a minimum of 25 percent of the product for a three-year period) and strong pressure to increase the percentage of local content (percentage of national integration, or PNI) in the products being produced.

Government incentives were offered to support local manufacture, primarily through a tax rebate certificate (called *CEPROFIS*). These could amount to as much as 15 percent in tax credits for either buyers of strategic capital goods or manufacturers who qualified through the acquisition of local parts and components. In order to qualify, the product must be listed on a strategic list, the company must be registered in a capital goods development program, the product must reach a level of 50 percent PNI within a negotiated number of years (more relaxed standards for the new and strategic minicomputer program unveiled in late 1981), the company must be located in a priority zone in accordance with the NIDP priorities, and, finally, the company must be 51 percent Mexican owned.

With great fanfare, the government introduced a program that required the huge parastatal enterprises to give preference to capital goods produced in Mexico for their massive capital investment/expansion programs. Observers who closely follow the capital investment forecasts of the parastatals appreciated the significant incentive to new investment that such preference could conceivably constitute—particularly in view of the enormous capital requirements to develop a capital goods industry in Mexico. Joint committees were established, composed of representatives of the parastatals (PEMEX, the Federal Electricity Corporation or CFE, the SIDERMEX steel conglomerate, and the others) and the corresponding national industrial chamber (from CONCAMIN, the National Confederation of Chambers of Industry) representing the private sector. These joint public/private sector committees were to have overseen the program's implementation.

Criticism from the Mexican private sector, however, has pointed out the committees' shortcomings. In addition to imposing unrealistic export requirements on Mexican industries that are not yet efficient enough to meet international competition, these joint committees have either been suspended (in the case of PEMEX) or have never functioned at all. Thus Mexican entrepreneurs have complained that the Mexican parastatals are continuing to import foreign-made capital equipment—to the detriment of the strategic national capital goods program. The Mexican executives' criticisms, especially with respect to unrealistic exports, contained the seeds of suggestions that led to the 1984 indirect modifications in Mexicanization requirements.

PRACTICAL APPROACHES: BOLSA MEXICANIZATION

Faced with Mexicanization requirements that seasoned observers believe will be imposed again when the fiscal crisis abates, a foreign company can look at several alternatives for creating a joint venture through divesting 51 percent of its wholly owned Mexican subsidiary. One approach, identified very early in this process, was the possibility of selling shares on the Mexican stock exchange (BOLSA) to comply with the requirements of local ownership. In fact this approach has been successfully undertaken by several U.S. companies, including prominent firms in food and chemicals industries, among others. The NFIC, however, took the position that control does not pass to Mexican nationals in a public stock offering of 51 percent of the shares of the Mexican company when a single or related foreign investor holds the substantial block of foreign shares (49 percent, or perhaps 40 percent).

The NFIC refers to this as "atomization" of the Mexican shares, a technique used to diffuse the power of individual shareholders. Although no challenge to publicly held companies has been made by the governmental authorities, it is understood that new applications for public offerings under those circumstances have not been approved by the National Securities Commission, and the NFIC representative now sits on the Securities Commission.

In recent years, a number of proposals have been introduced to strengthen the capital markets in Mexico and build investor protection for domestic capital formation. Indeed, the lack of confidence of Mexican investors has been apparent in both the 1976 and 1982 devaluations, preceding each of which the parity between the peso and the U.S. dollar deteriorated sharply. A major priority, present at the highest level of government planning, is to stabilize the capital markets to maintain the confidence of Mexican investors.

As new improvements are introduced to strengthen the capital markets, and as creative approaches to structure public offerings are defined, one can envision scenarios in which small groups of Mexican investors emerge with enough power to gain effective control. Various control techniques are known in sophisticated Mexican business and financial circles, but have not yet been implemented on any large scale.

OTHER DIVESTMENT ALTERNATIVES

Other alternatives for divesting 51 percent of a wholly owned company include traditional approaches to finding one or more

Mexican partners to acquire the foreign shares. There is no single approach that will be preferable in all situations, and the evaluation must consider the peculiar characteristics of the industry, the firm's competitive position, capital requirements, and other factors. Among the first potential partners to be considered are the distributors, customers, and suppliers of the existing company. If the company sells its products or services to one of the parastatals, that "partnership" option is frequently examined, sometimes at the request of the Mexican government.

Joint ventures with Mexican government entities are not uncommon in several basic industries, including automotive parts, trucks, farm equipment, chemicals, and even engineering. Traditional Mexican government banks and formerly private banks have become increasingly active in industrial development and have recently been taking a more active and direct role in the management of companies in which they previously took more passive equity positions.

More sophisticated options for forming a 51 percent Mexican partnership involve the combination of a parastatal enterprise and a bank, or a bank and a private Mexican company. Of course, the most common alternative is finding a Mexican company that will acquire the 51 percent needed to comply with Mexicanization requirements.

U.S. companies already operating in a joint venture form in Mexico are more frequently facing other problems: what to do when "irreconcilable differences" arise with the existing Mexican government or private partner, or what must be done when the existing Mexican partner, due to financial difficulties, informs the U.S. firm that they are unable to continue with the enterprise. The use of Mexican trusts *(Fideicomisos)* has become increasingly popular in recent years. In fact, the trust is mentioned in Articles Eighteen through Twenty-Three of the FIL, and regulated in some detail by Resolution 9.

More and more foreign companies have faced the obligation under an NFIC directive to place 51 percent (or more) of their shares in a trust with a qualified Mexican financial institution and have been given a limited period of time to locate a suitable joint venture partner. The trust device, of course, is only an interim solution. But it should be approached with long-term goals in mind.

Although reactions will vary with the current policy of the top government authorities, many middle- and senior-level officials of the ministries most directly regulating foreign investment are aware of the complexities of successfully operating a joint venture company. Thus, on several occasions, companies have been successful in securing extensions. These companies presented a well-prepared and logical explanation of their long-term plans and emphasized that successful implementation would depend on finding the proper partner. Preparation is the key word.

The longer term approach to solving complex problems has been in favor in recent years. Government officials now view indirect solutions, such as the "pyramiding of enterprises," as an attempt to evade Mexican law and policy. In late 1981, the NFIC issued an amendment to Resolution 11 that purported to specifically disapprove the pyramid device. The constitutional basis of the NFIC's position has been questioned by leading law firms in Mexico, and there appears to be a division of opinion among leading Mexican corporate lawyers. In any event, even if the amended resolution were to be successfully challenged, the important message is that the NFIC is aware of the tactic, disapproves of same, and will strive to find ways of securing compliance with its objectives for the benefit of the nation.

Finally, although the subject of selecting a joint venture partner will be treated in more depth in the next chapter, it is important, at this point, to note the pitfalls involved in one commonly used approach. I refer to the tendency to gravitate toward the largest industrial groups in Mexico as joint venture partners. Well-publicized developments related to one such group, previously the largest in Mexico, are an unfortunate example of why U.S. firms must revise this nearsighted strategy.

This Mexican group, whose name has now become a household word in U.S. international business circles, entered into a large number of joint ventures in nontraditional areas of its business in the past few years. The group publicly attributes its current difficult financial position to continued high interest rates on many of its foreign currency loans. (The Mexican government, through BANOBRAS, a government bank, is reported to own in excess of 70 percent of the group's equity, and even the group's core business and largest cash cow is rumored to be the subject of negotiations at this writing.)

High interest rates notwithstanding, classical management analysts have been quick to point out that this kind of aggressive expansion into a large number of nontraditional businesses leaves the company without many of the tools to manage any sort of a business crisis and, simultaneously, with little, if any, common corporate language. Most likely, a combination of these factors, aggravated by the triple devaluation of the peso, resulted in the group's financial difficulties.

Thus, the process of locating suitable joint venture partners in Mexico should be carried out with the use of competent advisers who are thoroughly familiar with Mexican law and business practice. Compatibility of the U.S. firm in terms of size, experience, corporate style, and business culture in general are important prerequisites for a cross-cultural corporate marriage. Brazilian experts have suggested that the average life of a joint venture in that country may be between six and seven years. In Mexico it is all very new—and the jury is still out—but already the casualty list is growing.

2

New Joint Ventures for Manufacturing Companies

The exasperating frustrations and difficulties encountered in exporting industrial or commercial products into the Mexican market have pushed many manufacturing companies toward a joint venture decision.

Certainly, problems abound. There are, for example, plenty of stories—some of them quite colorful—about shipments being delayed or stopped at the customs office at border locations. Likewise, the problems in managing or terminating a distributor are important—and expensive. Both these hardships, however, are somewhat outside the subject area of this monograph.

Many exporters face a problem that has completely different dimensions: Their distributor, importer, or local affiliate reports that the import license required to bring the products into Mexico has been denied—or that an import license has been approved but for a limited quantity and/or limited period.

As more products, assemblies, subassemblies, and systems are produced locally, in line with higher "Mexican content" requirements (as now apply in the automotive industry, for example), and as secondary petrochemical plants go onstream as a result of the policy of increased processing of local raw materials, more companies will face this problem. It is directly related to the import policy and customs regulations. The financial crisis, which resulted in a drastic curtailment of imports during 1982-84 (this writing), has exacerbated this trend.

MEXICAN IMPORT POLICY AND "CLOSED BORDERS"

The Ministry of Commerce in Mexico maintains a product classification schedule, using the Brussels nomenclature system as modified by the Latin American Integration Association (formerly Latin American Free Trade Association or LAFTA). Duties are assigned to product categories, as is the usual practice. Mexico has traditionally maintained a system of prior approval (import licenses) for importation from abroad. A liberalization trend during the Lopez Portillo Administration (1976-82) led to the passage of a series of laws and decrees, beginning in 1978, the result of which was to eliminate the requirement of prior approval on a significantly high percentage of all products to be imported . (perhaps as much as 70 to 80 percent). With the removal of the import license requirement, however, came a corresponding increase in the actual duty levied on the product. This was for revenue-raising purposes—and to decrease the likelihood that a flood of imports would enter the market and injure domestic manufacturers, many of whom had been operating inefficiently with excess capacity and inadequate productivity, but remained profitable because of the government's protectionist policies.

The Secretariat of Commerce approves or denies an import license. In making this determination, the secretariat maintains close liaison with Mexican Chambers of Industry and Commerce through the National Confederation of Chambers of Industry (CONCAMIN) and Commerce (CONCANACO). These industry (private-sector) organizations maintain product committees which are broken down by product groups, subgroups, and classes (committees and subcommittees). The practical effect was and is that when an application is presented to the Ministry for an import license, the Ministry seeks advice from the committees. Sitting on the committees would be the competitors of the U.S. exporter. Their inclination, of course, is to indicate that the product is previously available in Mexico—adequate justification for denial of the application for the import license.

Government policy in this regard is aimed, first, at protecting products presently being manufactured in Mexico and, second, at protecting products being assembled in Mexico. Finally, manufacturers of products not otherwise available in Mexico find approval of their import license applications facilitated if their advocates in the hearings can establish this condition to the satisfaction of the Ministry of Commerce.

The entire approval process highlights the importance of being extremely specific in identifying the particular classification or product for which the import license is being requested. Pumps and valves are frequently used to illustrate this point. As any industry source can affirm, there are literally hundreds of varieties of each of these common items on the market. We are familiar with many instances in which an application for a license for a particular pump, a sophisticated flow-metering pump, for example, has been denied based on the representation of "Mexican manufacture" by a local company. In actuality, the local firm produced a much simplified pump, totally inadequate for the purpose desired. The same scenario has been the case with a wide variety of other products. Any company seeking approval of an import license simply cannot overlook the importance of direct participation in the deliberations and the necessity of differentiating carefully among products.

When a product is determined by officials in various Mexican government ministries to be adequately supplied by Mexican sources in sufficient quantity to meet the existing demands, the result is the denial of applications for importation of these products. This is referred to informally as "closing the border."

In view of the Mexican Foreign Investment Law (FIL) discussed earlier, the U.S. manufacturer is faced with a dilemma: form a joint venture to manufacture the products in Mexico in compliance with the FIL, or be progressively shut out of the

Mexican market. The decision is made: form a joint venture in Mexico. The requirement: find a suitable partner.

This decision is almost entirely defensive, and all too often the quality of commitment to making the venture successful reflects a defensive stance. This need not be the case.

Adopting an offensive strategy does *not* mean, however, resorting to any of those devices (sometimes examined and even used) for avoiding the full impact of the FIL. Such tactics include, for example, issuance of shares of the new joint venture in the name of passive shareholders who merely lend their name in order to qualify under the FIL. This procedure, known as a *"prestanombre"* (the straw-man concept), is expressly illegal under the FIL. In addition, there are important practical matters. We are aware of cases where the so-called "passive investor" did not remain silent after the company was incorporated and operating. In that situation, the U.S. investor has no legal remedies, since he participated in a willful violation of the FIL.

THE SEARCH FOR A JOINT VENTURE PARTNER

As indicated earlier, U.S. companies new to Mexico tend to identify the largest Mexican "supergroups" as potential joint venture partners without realizing the rather formidable disadvantages that may accompany these particular groups, as anyone who had entered into such an arrangement with the industrial group referred to earlier now sadly knows. Futhermore, these supergroups have been deluged with propositions from U.S., Japanese, German, English, French, Italian, Spanish, Canadian, Dutch, and other foreign companies.

The partner selection process is the second most critical element in a successful formula for establishing a new joint venture in Mexico, either manufacturing or service, subordinated only to the true commitment that the management of the firm has made. The process should be undertaken with the assistance of experienced advice, considerable patience, and realistic expectations. Moreover, management should be ready to modify these expectations several times during the process—and afterwards. On average, about two years are needed from the time the decision is made until the company is established and work initiated.

WHAT TO LOOK FOR

U.S. companies invariably come to the negotiating table with some technology that has served them well in the domestic market, as well as in the markets of more industrialized countries around the world. In addition to the question of size (large company vs. small company), it is vital to search for a company with a more or less comparable or complementary organization. Although this will depend on product, industry, technology, and competition, the ideal prospect would be a Mexican group that is not totally dominating nor totally passive, as a portfolio investor theoretically may be. The Mexican partner should have strengths to operate effectively in the culturally distinct Mexican market, and sufficient access to adequate financial resources.

Manufacturing

Manufacturing capability, of course, would be a critical element in the criteria used to judge a target company. This should include high-quality product orientation and reputation for reliability and service. A quantitative and qualitative analysis of the physical facilities and capabilities should be involved. If they have never "cut metal" before, why should they be your partner now?

Marketing

The marketing organization should be evaluated carefully to review its domestic capability as well as its potential for international marketing, if appropriate. This latter element is, however, another important asset that the U.S. company brings to the negotiating table, and may also be a control point.

Human Resources

Human resources are vital, and at this stage in Mexico's industrial growth, are a critical bottleneck. This translates into a need for experienced key-management personnel, including manufacturing, labor relations, marketing, accounting, and finance. In evaluating key personnel, don't overlook the importance of adequate English-language capability. The simple ability to communicate with the counterpart in the U.S. company's home office has made a significant difference in a number of the joint ventures in which we have been involved. And the absence of that ability is a frequent cause of disaster. There are several good recruiting firms in Mexico to facilitate the process of staffing the joint venture itself, at the first stage.

Government and Industry Contacts

Finally, the question of government contacts is usually raised very early in the deliberation process. You should not *overestimate* the value of this element. We may suggest however, that almost anyone who is now operating successfully in Mexico probably has the requisite contacts in the government ministries, as well as with the parastatal organizations, and quite likely the labor unions and the principal political party in the country (the Institutional Revolutionary Party or PRI). Spend more time looking at the potential partner's industry contacts, which can help you get an idea of their reputation.

Conflicts of Interest

Other factors include cross-cultural elements such as the philosophy on conflicts of interest or "corporate opportunities" for the principals involved. The potential partner is very likely involved in other investments in Mexico at the same time, as are other members of the family. In cases where the partner is dominated by a single, strong individual, the question should be asked: What plans have been made for succession in the event of accident or death? Finally, the question of control and how it can be divided should be a major discussion point in the negotiations.

Forming the JV Company

The formation of a permanent joint venture company is similar to the normal establishment of any other Mexican company —with additional complexities due to the nature of the relationship. Forming a JV calls for the preparation of Articles of Incorporation, which define (largely under Mexican law) all the usual matters: name, duration, domicile, and purpose of the corporation; the capital and classes of shares; the issuance, ownership, and transfer of shares; changes in the capital (increases and reductions); the shareholders' meetings and notice therefor; directors' meetings and notice therefor; the powers of and limitations on the directors and officers; the independent inspectors; and liquidation or dissolution of the company.

The three principal issues to be examined in the establishment of any joint venture are (1) *participation* (who contributes what resources and gets how many shares in return), (2) *management* (which partner appoints the general manager or managing director and other key "directors or managers"), and (3) *control* (usually thought of in terms of voting control in both the shareholders' and directors' meetings, with a particular emphasis on the protection that the minority partner maintains in the form of vetoes over the most important issues). From my experience with the agreements associated with joint ventures in Mexico, management and control by the U.S. minority shareholder are best maintained through a combination of affirmative and negative controls. These characteristics should be programmed into the search.

DIVIDING CONTROL INTO ITS CONSTITUENT ELEMENTS

After the determinations of initial capital contribution and equity percentages are made, the issues of management and control normally occupy the bulk of the negotiations. The question of control should be broken down into a number of constituent units. For example, financial control is usually addressed at the outset. One could divide financial control into the familiar treasury function and the accounting function (roughly comparable to the treasurer/comptroller dichotomy in U.S. corporations). Technological control can be divided into the manufacturing itself (production), quality control, and the actual technical direction, which may involve engineering and development.

Both supply and distribution are also vital elements of control. Control over human resources and government relations are sometimes addressed, but often overlooked. The latter functions are normally managed by the Mexican partner, as may be the former, depending on the partner's experience.

It's not unreasonable to suggest that if you are able to maintain control over purchasing (supply of parts, raw materials, and so on), distribution (including a strong influence over domestic sales and control over international marketing), and the technology itself, the net result would be effective control. U.S. companies always ask for financial control, which may, in fact, be neither necessary nor reasonable. One could make a strong case for a good Mexican executive carrying the financial responsibilities, including credit negotiations with Mexican banks. A deputy financial director can usually serve the purposes of the U.S. company in terms of the financial controls normally required.

U.S. companies invariably ask that their accounting system be imposed on the Mexican company. In our experience, this is an unreasonable demand—one that's usually rejected. Rather, the U.S. company should carefully review the Mexican partner's existing accounting system and creatively form building blocks to make the transition for accounting reporting purposes.

GOVERNMENT RELATIONS

Many U.S. companies have made the mistake of leaving to their

Mexican partners the management of government relations. We recommend that the Mexican partner should take the lead in these matters through the management of the joint venture company itself. But those U.S. executives responsible for the investment should make a substantial effort to understand exactly which ministries, agencies, and bureaus are involved in the approval process, as well as some of the key individuals to be encountered. This is particularly true with respect to incentives under the NIDP and the implementing regulations thereof, and anything connected with the Ministries of Finance, Energy and Mining, Interior, Commerce, and possibly others.

The process of negotiating for export commitments, if any are involved, and concessionary financing should also be thoroughly understood. All too often, U.S. companies leave these matters in the hands of outside law firms. Visualize, for a moment, how officials in the ministry perceive this process. The officials see the faces of the same highly qualified and experienced Mexican lawyers on a daily basis, each lawyer representing a range of different foreign companies. These officials have expressed repeatedly their desire to make direct contact with the foreign and local principals involved. Certainly, foreign investors should use local counsel—but in an advisory capacity and not as the principal emissary of the manufacturing firm itself. This may also be an indication of the U.S. investor's lack of commitment.

MEXICAN BUSINESS CULTURE

U.S. companies invariably underestimate the time required to gain an intimate or at least a working knowledge of the Mexican business system, the private-sector groups, the federal government, the labor unions, and the extremely important interrelationships between these groups and the PRI. Relationships and processes differ sharply from those in the U.S., for example, and in European countries. Understanding those differences is vital.

Also, U.S. companies must develop the ability to listen to propositions made by their counterparts—where they intend to go and how they plan to get there. Junior and many senior North American executives who are somewhat inexperienced in dealing with foreign cultures are aware of the need to be courteous and often overcompensate in this regard. They frequently confuse the necessity of courtesy with the requirement for sincere, candid, and straightforward negotiations and discussions from the outset.

Courtesy, of course, is important. It's essential. But "straight talk" is equally essential, and frank discussions are vital. It's not impolite to ask tough questions. For example, you've undoubtedly calculated the level of productivity you hope to attain, once the plant is in operation. But achieving those objectives depends, in part, on the drive possessed by and management rights given to those in line positions. Dealing with this issue demands that tough questions be asked.

The same principle holds for achieving expected sales figures. Given the existing shortage of capable line and middle-management personnel in Mexico, and the infringement on management rights arising from the Mexican labor relations system, this is an important problem area for manufacturing companies.

Foreign investors should also understand Mexico's approach to technology transfer arrangements (primarily licensing of patents, trademarks, know-how, or a combination, plus technical assistance and management contracts). Many U.S. companies assume they will get royalties and technical assistance fees at levels comparable to those in the U.S. and Europe. This is not the case. Most readers will be familiar with the Mexican Law on Transfer of Technology (effective in 1973) and the Law on Inventions and Trademarks (effective in 1976). A new Law on Transfer of Technology, published on January 11, 1982, and effective on February 10, supersedes the 1973 law. In addition to prior approval and registration requirements and the list of disfavored clauses, this law also regulates royalty and technical assistance fee rates through the review process by the National Registry of Technology Transfer (NRTT). The NRTT is part of the same bureau in the Secretariat of Commerce that controls foreign investment.

Experience with the NRTT over the eleven years of its existence suggests that, generally speaking, the foreign licensor can expect a royalty rate of 3 percent at maximum, and 1 percent or less with a bare trademark license. In fact, with licensing arrangements from the foreign firm to its minority-owned joint venture company, the NRTT takes the position that the foreign minority shareholder will be rewarded for its investment through dividends. Under Mexican law, dividends are not limited to a percentage of registered capital (before incurring either a super-tax or disapproval entirely), as they are in Brazil, Argentina, Venezuela, and elsewhere. With the new exchange controls, dividends in Mexico may be remitted (assuming dollars are available on the free market) after the new aggregate corporate and dividend tax has been paid on earnings.

Another practical factor is worth mentioning. The Mexican partner's reaction to the technology royalties varies according to the size and muscle of the company. But the larger Mexican groups all take the position that if the U.S. investor insists on a technology royalty, they will take a management (contract) fee equivalent to the technology fees, since they are providing management services.

PROTECTION OF MINORITY INTERESTS

Opinions differ sharply over whether Mexican law truly protects the rights of minority foreign shareholders. The Mexican Corporation Law (part of the Commercial Code), read in conjunction with the FIL, would suggest that such protections are limited in terms of legal remedies. The nomination of an outside inspector (*comisario*) for the minority shareholder is one such protection. The *comisario* serves as a nonvoting member of the board of directors, which is often an active management group in Mexican companies. In larger joint venture companies, management operating committees are also common. The Corporation Law also requires an extraordinary meeting of shareholders for discussion of a specified list of major policy-type issues, and the extraordinary meeting requires 75 percent of the shareholders represented on the first quorum call to be valid. This percentage, however, reverts to the normal 51 percent on subsequent quorum calls, and thus does not offer much protection.

But the position taken in recent years by the bureaucrats is generally reasonable. These joint venture companies require mutual agreement to be effective, and the government officials are well aware of this. Thus, in practice, it is common to negotiate arrangements for veto rights over a considerable number of important matters at the board level, and receive approval for these agreements from the bureau.

As was mentioned earlier, however, control is usually maintained by a combination of affirmative and negative controls. Experience to date suggests that in the case of successful joint ventures in Mexico, the negative controls (veto rights) are generally used more to help justify approval of the investment and subsequent capital increases in the U.S. firm's internal management discussions before top management gives its approval. Operating control is more often developed and actually shared as the partners become better acquainted. If important issues are being decided by the closeness of the vote at board or shareholders' meetings, that joint venture is already in serious trouble.

COMMITMENT

We've had executives come to us with instructions to organize a joint venture in Mexico within six months so they can move on to a new project in the Pacific Basin or elsewhere. Our advice: Forget Mexico! Such requests reflect a defensive strategy rather than an aggressive approach to the realities of the Mexican marketplace, and inadequate commitment.

Certainly, financial resources must be addressed and the requirements for future capitalization attended to, as needs develop. But the U.S. firm simply cannot afford to underestimate the importance of management resources and continuity. A commitment to providing high-quality management talent for assignment to the Mexican venture is critical to success, and those assigned must be allowed enough time to do the job right.

Most U.S. and Mexican executives repeatedly emphasize that the bedrock of a successful joint venture operation is integrity, trust, and mutual respect. They frequently talk about the requirement for a clarity of objectives; of communication between partners at various levels as well as from the joint venture company to each partner; of clearly defined management authority; of operating goals, requirements, and reports; and of joint planning, goal setting, and actual sharing of management. They underscore that it is essential to establish solid working rapport at multiple levels from the outset. From all of our own direct and indirect experience, I have concluded that compatible "corporate cultures" are highly desirable, if not essential.

TECHNOLOGY

Many U.S. companies assume they can contribute their technology as their share of the capital contribution and avoid the necessity of a significant cash investment. Picture, for a moment, the U.S. investor offering to contribute technology, the Mexican investor offering land and buildings, and both sides believing no significant cash will be required. The result: an absence of working capital to purchase raw materials, supplies, parts, capital equipment, and other necessities (not to mention heat, light, power, and other overhead expenses), or to pay salaries. This approach is totally unrealistic, no matter how valuable the technology is. That technology, together with manufacturing, quality and service, a good knowledge of the local market, and local financing may make a complete package. But there should be enough working capital to carry the company well beyond normal sales collection cycles; start-up delays and problems are commonplace, and receivables take much longer to collect in Mexico than in the U.S.

3

New Joint Ventures for Service Companies

U.S. companies providing a wide range of services for infrastructure and the process industries have been attracted to Mexico for many years. And for good reasons. Consider the tremendous amount of new plant construction, port expansion, and modernization and expansion of railroads, steel and petrochemical complexes, and power generating facilities required in Mexico. These service companies, however, find themselves facing problems similar to those encountered by manufacturing firms.

Traditionally, service companies have been able to operate in a number of areas—architecture, engineering, design, construction management, and international procurement, for example—without forming a legal entity in the recipient country or paying taxes there. But the days of protected contracts have almost come to an end. Most developing countries now require international firms to qualify some kind of an entity locally—perhaps even pre-qualify with the agency or ministry involved. Moreover, service companies now pay income taxes and, in some cases, other taxes as well. The competition is increasing and the operating conditions have been tightened.

OPTIONS FOR SALES OF SERVICES TO MEXICO

At first glance, there appear to be four different options available for foreign companies to perform services in Mexico:

- Direct prime contracting from the U.S. (or elsewhere).
- Subcontracting from the U.S. (or elsewhere).
- Establishing a Mexican branch.
- Establishing a Mexican company.

Closer inspection will reveal that the "closed border" phenomenon applies in the service industries in a different way, but with the same result.

Direct Prime Contracting from the U.S.

Traditionally, U.S. architecture, engineering, consulting, and construction companies have been able to enter into prime contracts with Mexican clients without having to establish a branch or subsidiary there. In recent years, however, the regulations of the "parastatal enterprises," such as Petroleos Mexicanos, S.A. (PEMEX), the Federal Electricity Corporation (CFE), the Mexican steel corporation (SIDERMEX), the state-owned railroad and telephone companies (FERROCARRILE and TELEFONOS), and others, have specified that these government enterprises shall have preference to Mexican companies in the award of their contracts. Only when the capability simply does not exist in Mexico will a foreign contractor be considered. In those cases, the foreign contractor is generally required to establish a legal entity in Mexico. At minimum, the foreigner must be registered as an international supplier to the government. This will also subject the foreign company to the Mexican Foreign Investment Law, which requires forming a joint venture.

In addition, the 1981 amendments to the tax law have significantly changed the tax consequences of work being performed inside and outside Mexico. This will also be discussed in more detail below, but if the company is deemed to have a "permanent establishment," the tax consequences will be identical to those for a Mexican corporation. With respect to construction, installation, maintenance, or assembly on immovable (real) property, the permanent establishment will be deemed to exist when such services or activities have a duration of more than 365 days. This contributes to the push toward a joint venture.

Subcontracting from the U.S.

Most U.S. service companies prefer to perform work in Mexico in a joint venture as a prime contractor. However, should the occasion arise where a Mexican company is awarded work and the foreign firm is requested to perform as a subcontractor, essentially the same consequences (tax liabilities) would apply as in the previous paragraph. This option, however, is less frequently available.

Establishing a Mexican Branch

The next alternative frequently investigated is the possibility of establishing a branch in Mexico in order to create some kind of a "permanent presence" that would not be subject to the FIL. That law, as described earlier, specifies the conditions under which any "foreign investor" may participate in the national economy, and the definition of foreign investor does extend to include foreign service companies with very little "investment." To my knowledge, however, no new branches of foreign corporations have been approved since 1973. In view of the variety of construction and engineering firms all over Mexico, it's difficult to envision any company successfully persuading the NFIC that its services are distinctive enough to deserve exception to the law. However, the NFIC may (as in Venezuela) provide authorization limited to a single project in special cases. For tax purposes, this special office would be treated as if it were a branch.

Establishing a Mexican Company

Once the possibility of a branch is eliminated, the next option involves the formation of a Mexican company. Traditionally, U.S. service companies also prefer to establish wholly owned subsidiaries abroad. Although the FIL prohibits the establishment of new companies in Mexico with greater than a 49 percent foreign equity participation, there have been rare cases in which the NFIC has approved a higher percentage due to extraordinary circumstances. The criteria for these exceptions are now well known and are included in the 1984 guidelines. Unfortunately, however, most fact situations do not qualify as an exception to the general rule, and I am unaware of *any* exceptions made for service companies, especially the usual one about the unique nature of your organization and its experience. As in Brazil, the government wants you to transfer some of that experience to a Mexican company.

Therefore, and in compliance with the FIL, the foreign firm must join in the establishment of a new Mexican joint venture company with its equity participation limited to 49 percent. This could, in turn, be treated in one of two ways: as a minority equity position in the Mexican company or as a "true" joint venture. The difference is that in the latter there is an *actual* "sharing" of management. And there are very carefully prepared approaches to allocating control among the two parties according to the strengths and weaknesses of each, analogous to the earlier discussions about manufacturing companies. In accordance with the FIL and policy, "management" or visible control of the entity must belong to Mexicans. This, of course, varies substantially according to the circumstances. The kind of partner you want, however, knows and respects your experience and wants you to take the lead in those areas.

TYPES OF JOINT VENTURES

There are essentially two different types of joint ventures that one could consider establishing. The normal entity is a "permanent" joint venture involving the establishment of a corporation with 51 percent of the equity divided among one *or more* Mexican shareholders and 49 percent (or less, if desired) owned by the

U.S. shareholder. The other alternative is a contract (project) or nonequity joint venture.

Equity Joint Ventures

When a services firm decides to establish a permanent presence to perform work in Mexico, it must establish a local company like a manufacturing firm (see discussion, Chapter 2). Effective control can, however, operate through the engineering control on the basis of the foreign company's experience and reputation—and the lack of same by the local partner. For example, you control engineering, construction management (CM), and international procurement, and they control labor, government relations, construction, and local procurement. Of course, the other common option is for the owner to bring in an American CM along with a strong Mexican construction group.

Non-Equity Joint Ventures

The major differences between permanent and temporary joint ventures are the term and the purpose. In this case, the territory for bidding on projects would be the same (at least initially, the Republic of Mexico), although the partners to the venture could agree to bid on projects outside of Mexico if it were to their mutual advantage. In a short-term joint venture, there have been arrangements in which the two parties agree that certain types of projects may be undertaken by one without the other in the event that one of the partners prefers not to bid on a particular project, to a particular client, or under other specified conditions (fixed price or lump-sum jobs, for example). In such cases, alternative teaming arrangements can be agreed upon.

The allocation of functions, administration and management, financing (both short-term and long-term), costs, and risk are other considerations that become more important in a nonequity joint venture. For those U.S. companies that have participated in such arrangements in any developing country, no further elaboration is required.

LOCAL TAX CONSIDERATIONS FOR SERVICE COMPANIES

Although this is not a detailed discussion on the Mexican tax consequences of doing business in Mexico, it is appropriate to identify at least some of the most important taxes that will apply to the joint venture's operations in Mexico.

General Income Taxes on Corporations

The Mexican Corporate Income Tax was, until recently, applied on a sliding scale, up to a maximum of 42 percent on the net taxable income of the corporation (gross income less allowable deductions). There is also a profit-sharing provision under the present Mexican Law requiring the employer to contribute 8 percent of pretax earnings to a fund, to be distributed to employees in accordance with prescribed criteria. Finally, there was traditionally a 21 percent withholding tax on dividends declared by Mexican corporations and remitted abroad (that is, to the U.S. shareholder). The change effective in 1984 is the substitution of an aggregate corporate and dividend withholding tax at a rate of up to 55 percent, possibly to be reduced after the crisis abates.

Other Taxes on Services

Most services joint ventures will be obliged to call upon their existing U.S. organization for specialized services for which the capability does not yet exist in Mexico, and for which economic factors dictate some delay before it will. This has important Mexican (and U.S.) tax implications. There is a 21 percent tax on the gross income from Mexican sources for services performed outside Mexico. In previous years, this tax was notorious and was referred to as the tax on technical services performed outside Mexico, or "technical services tax." Until 1980, the tax was 42 percent on gross income. In that year the local tax laws were changed to provide the option of either a 21 percent tax on gross income or a 42 percent tax on net income (gross income less allowable deductions). However, since many expenses incurred outside Mexico were generally not allowable as deductions, most companies elected the former option. There are certain exceptions to this. In the past, various arrangements were structured (involving rulings from the Mexican Treasury Department) which dramatically increased the foreign contractor's allowable deductions for expenses incurred outside Mexico, thereby reducing Mexican taxes. These rulings were generally limited to projects for state entities.

The 1981 Mexican Income Tax Law contains some very important changes. The technical services tax rate of 42 percent is still applied on services performed abroad, less allowable deductions, but the new law provides that deductions against gross may be taken regardless of where the expenses are incurred, with specific exceptions, if they are related to the source of the Mexican income and if the taxpayer maintains an authorized representative in Mexico who must comply with certain requirements and formalities. Generally accepted accounting records will suffice as substantiation for the expenses, even when incurred outside Mexico. For U.S. tax purposes, it should be noted that if such services are performed in the U.S., they do not qualify as generating foreign source income. Thus, even though Mexican taxes must be paid on such income, the foreign tax credit is not available for such taxes because of the limitation.

Alternatively, there is a 30 percent tax on gross income for construction, installation, or maintenance services performed by nonresident companies (that is, companies without a Mexican domicile, or a "permanent establishment"), which means the foreign parent company or other foreign affiliate providing the specialized services.

For 1981, construction companies were still permitted to elect the option of a 3.75 percent tax on gross construction revenues. However, this provision expired on January 1, 1982. As usual, a new set of substantial changes to the Tax Law was proposed late in 1981 and became effective on January 1, 1982. In recent years virtually every annual amendment to the tax laws affects these types of operations.

Permanent Establishment

The 1981 change introduced the concept of "permanent establishment"—a most important change. Nonresident companies that fit into this category are taxed on all income attributed to their permanent establishments. A "permanent establishment" is defined as any place of business used partially or totally to engage in business activities, and includes branches, offices, installations, or a variety of other similar concepts. As indicated earlier, a special test has been created for certain construction-related activities. With respect to construction, installation, maintenance, or assembly services on immovable property (real estate), or inspection activities related to the same, the permanent establishment will be deemed to exist when such services or activities have a duration of more than 365 days.

If a permanent establishment is deemed to exist, taxation is similar to that applied to a branch. Those Mexican branches that still exist are taxed like a Mexican corporation with the addition of a 21 percent tax on branch profits (similar to the 21 percent withholding tax on dividends) even if the branch profits are not remitted to the foreign parent. The net result again appears to be a push toward "encouraging" foreign services companies to organize Mexican joint ventures.

Asociacion en Participacion (A en P)

A commonly used form of joint venture for a specific project is what they call an *Asociacion en Participacion* (A en P). In this arrangement, the Mexican partner *(asociante)* is like a general partner and must comply with all obligations under Mexican law. The foreign partner *(asociado)* may characterize the services he will furnish from the A en P (inside Mexico) as a capital contribution and consequences will flow from that. This form, when coupled with the permanent establishment concept, results in some tax effects that approximate normal corporate tax rates.

There are some other provisions in the tax laws that may provide interesting possibilities for tax and financial planning for service/joint ventures. For example, interest payments to a foreign parent company were subject to a 42 percent withholding tax. For tax planning purposes, it has been advantageous on occasion for some companies to receive some payments as interest in addition to the dividend. Interest payments to foreign banks are subject to a 15 percent withholding tax rate (assuming the foreign bank is registered in Mexico), which is less than the 21 percent rate formerly applied to dividends. The foreign bank could lend money to the Mexican company directly (probably with a guarantee from the parent company), although the interest rate is limited to 2 percent over the London Inter-Bank Offering Rate (LIBOR) as of the date of contracting the loan, and this may not be attractive to the banks. In addition, from time to time, with high inflation and an unstable peso, assuming dollar loan obligations is not recommended for Mexican companies and there is usually a short supply of peso financing.

In April of 1982, the Bank of Mexico (Central Bank) announced important modifications to its "swaps" loan program, which, when in effect, may also provide planning possibilities. Finally, there are some attractive provisions for "financial" leasing, as withholding is made only against that portion of the payment considered as interest. For those service companies providing equipment and personnel for a combined daily rate, separating them may sometimes be advantageous.

These are classic examples of why these joint venture companies need an experienced financial director to take advantage of all possible forms of concessionary or advantageous local financing. All of the above suggestions will vary depending on currently prevailing conditions and policies, and Mexican tax advisers must be consulted.

RECOMMENDED APPROACH

Approach the Altar Carefully

Much more can and should be written about that form of international marriage known as a joint venture. Suffice it to say that there are a considerable number of consultants and others who offer, for various prices, different types of marriage brokerage services to assist U.S. companies in locating a partner in Mexico, especially in the engineering and construction business. There is no mystery to this process. But we strongly suggest that the process in Mexico is quite different from that in the Far East, and in developing countries in other parts of the world.

Not everyone is related to the "royal family" in Mexico, and having the director general of the parastatal customer as a direct or hidden partner may not help if he is suddenly sacked and sent off to Siberia. The process is much more similar to that in Brazil; Mexico is a large country (population approximating 75 million and projected to reach around 100 million by the turn of the century) with an increasingly diversified industrial base. You can find a wide variety of Mexican businessmen whose backgrounds may, alone or in conjunction with others, provide the right complement to your firm's resources. In addition, there is no shortage of Mexican investors with adequate capital.

Moreover, an increasing number of government banks with industrial divisions (run by former senior executives of industrial firms) now recruit highly qualified Mexican executives from private industry to run new joint ventures in which they become the 51 percent Mexican partner (or higher in specific cases). This is increasingly obvious with service companies of late, and we are aware of situations in which groups have been formed or tailored to meet the needs of specific situations.

One warning: Beware of those consultants who are all too ready to introduce you to someone who is or purports to be the brother (or cousin, or son) of the Mexican president, the director general of PEMEX, CFE, or the others, the mayor of Mexico City, or governor of a state, or one of their key advisers. Instead, use the more substantive approach detailed earlier. Of course, you hit the jackpot if the close friend or relative of the well-placed official also heads up a company with resources complementary to yours. But the line to his office is probably pretty long.

After selecting a partner, take the time to develop close working relationships at multiple levels. This means direct contact and "relationship building" between engineering, operations, accounting, finance, purchasing, and other important working departments as appropriate, in addition to CEO levels.

Limited Duration

Consider the establishment of the joint venture for a limited duration, initially. This permits the relationship to evolve while the parties work together on one or two smaller projects. Establishing the company can allow you to bid and execute projects jointly, but the company can then expire at the end of a specific period (for example, two or three years). This is much easier than going through a corporate divorce for noncompatibility. If the relationship works well, the duration can be extended for as long as you wish. If the company is allowed to terminate by expiration, the selection process can be repeated and a more compatible partner found. At the same time, you may be able to protect your reputation and the contacts you have developed.

CONCLUSION

Like a story, a joint venture has a beginning, a middle, and an end. All of those aspects should be considered at the outset, especially the divorce or termination provisions.

If the venture proves successful, either party should be able to extricate itself, but at a premium, representing the expected value. The reverse should be the case under conditions that appear to be unprofitable. The problem of resolution of disputes likely to arise among the "partners" should be considered, and reliable, objective means or formulas included to carry out the process. Such provisions in the agreement should not be "boiler-plate"; they should be tailored to the situation. Legal, financial, tax, and accounting advisers should be consulted before beginning the partner selection process, to help identify criteria which must be considered.

But the most important element of all, even superseding the partner to be selected, is the commitment: the willingness to pay the ante to play in the Mexican poker game. The stakes can be very attractive.